HOW TO **DOUBLE**
THE PROFITS
IN YOUR HAIR SALON

The Little Book That Makes Big Profits

Robin J. Elliott

LeverageAdvantage.com

HOW TO DOUBLE THE PROFITS IN YOUR HAIR SALON

The Little Book That Makes Big Profits

First Edition

Cover design/formatting: www.lighthousedesign.ca

ISBN: 978-0-9687713-2-7

Hair and Beauty Business

Elliott, Robin J., 1953 -

How to Double the Profits in Your Hair Salon
by Robin J. Elliott

Printed in the United States

"Hairdressers are a wonderful breed. You work one-on-one with another human being and the object is to make them feel so much better and to look at themselves with a twinkle in their eye."
~ Vidal Sassoon

Index

PHASE ONE
Foundation

PHASE TWO
All About SALES: Fill Your Chairs with the Right People

Preface

There's a story about a kid who claims that elves get into his room at night and steal his underpants. His parents don't believe him, but he insists, so they agree to hide in his room and await the mischievous elves. Eventually, around midnight, a motley band of elves climbs stealthily through the open window and commences to steal the boy's underpants out of his bottom drawer.

The father steps up and asks the head elf why they're stealing the underpants, and the elf replies that it's a new business that the elves have started. "But how can you make money by stealing underpants?" asks the bewildered dad. "Oh, we have a business plan," replies the pompous elf, "Step 1 – steal underpants. Step 3 – make a profit."

This booklet might be titled, Step Two for Hair Salon Owners.

Who Is This Booklet For?

Hair Salon Owners everywhere can learn from this powerful, practical, and profitable information.

The author has spent twenty-five years focused on collaborative, reciprocal marketing, and the ideas here, although principally gained from his experience serving thousands of salons in collaboration with large hair product companies like Redken, Wella, and Goldwell, includes information gleaned from a wide variety of other industries and a wealth of marketing experience.

By borrowing proven concepts and adopting winning systems from other industries, Robin J. Elliott has shared information that would cost thousands of dollars in this book. Mr. Elliott is also available to assist hair product companies to expand their market and add value to their customers.

The Author: Who Is Robin J. Elliott?

This is Robin J. Elliott's 15th and latest book. Instead of a lot of filler, his books are to the point, direct, and bottom-line oriented, packed with information that can be implemented fast, and in the language of the business owner. You will enjoy the fact that he is obviously on the cutting edge and up to date with what is happening in your industry. Learn more about him and sign up for his free weekly newsletter here: http://LeverageAdvantage.com.

This Book is Divided into Four Distinct and Important Sections:

Phase One (The Foundation, without which your building will collapse.)

Phase Two (Filling Your Chairs with the Right People. This has to happen in order for the next two Phases to work.)

Phase Three (Measure Everything. This has to happen in order to optimize Phases One and Four.)

Phase Four (The Magical Back End. You are now ready to supercharge your bottom line!)

The Challenge

A few of the common problems facing hair salons today:
1. Instead of buying products from your salon, clients are buying similar products and knock-offs at wholesale stores.

2. It's hard to get new clients and fill the chairs.

3. It's hard to get clients to spend more.

4. It's hard to get clients to refer their friends.

5. It's hard to get clients to visit the salon every six weeks.

6. It's hard to build loyalty in clients; hard to keep them – they seem only to be loyal to price or they follow their stylist when he or she leaves your salon to work somewhere else or start their own salons.

7. It's hard to get good stylists and keep them.

8. It's hard to differentiate yourself in the market, with new salons popping up like mushrooms. Competition, price cutting is hard to deal with.

9. "Our costs go up, but our prices don't!" (Shrinking profit margins.)

10. "I AM the salon – I can't sell it the way it is, because if I leave the salon will fail. And when I go on holiday, income shrinks and clients leave."

11. "Chicken or feathers, feast or famine - I make money during the busy times and use up all my savings / get into debt during the quiet times."

12. Limitations: geographic, political, weather, competition, legislation – much of which you cannot control.

This booklet provides solutions to the above.

The Objective

We're in business to make the maximum profit, not sales. We're not here to provide stylists or relatives with jobs. We don't want to compete on price. Ultimately, we would like to be able to sell our salon or salons for top dollar.

Let's discuss profit margins. No matter what your profit margin is on the products you sell, there is a cost involved in ordering and holding inventory, stacking shelves, time taken selling the product, theft, returns, labour.

And you have overhead – leases, employees, maintenance, insurance, hydro, phone, printing, Internet, flowers, and on and on - the "cost of doing business" - and all this eats away at the amount of money you put in your pocket at the end of every month. Even when times are quiet, the overheads don't go away; we still have to pay to keep the doors open.

The final NET PROFIT percentage in your salon is low. We want to fix that.

The Objective of this book is to increase your Bottom Line: Your Profit. When you sell your salon, the buyer will look at the PROFIT. That's why most of the ideas and solutions and suggestions in this book can be implemented with No Cost and No Risk. We want to protect, hold, and increase your bottom line at every juncture. And we want you to SYSTEMIZE your business, so that it runs well with you or without you.

Also, you need to set yourself apart from the competition out there so that price is no longer the deciding factor. And you need to learn how to create massive client and employee loyalty.

Finally, we want to smooth that yo-yo, runaway roller-coaster income out and avoid the "feast or famine" scenario. All this will reduce your stress levels, which increases your health and happiness and improves all your relationships.

When you're relaxed and supported with the right information, when you know how to reduce risk in your business, you will be more friendly and approachable, more creative, a better manager and stylist.

WARNING:

This booklet can help you double the profits in your hair salon, but please be aware of the following:

1. While we buy books with the best intentions, according to Jerold Jenkins of the Jenkins Group, 57 percent of new books are not read to completion. You need to commit to reading this book a few times, making copious notes in the margin, applying the ideas, and then moving to the next level.

2. A book won't change your life unless you meticulously make notes, apply and implement the ideas and solutions consistently, and get expert guidance and mentoring (from people who understand your industry) along the way when you get stuck or have questions.

3. Please make notes and don't rush through this book and assume you know everything there is to know. You will forget a lot of it if it's not repeated; that's simply human nature. A great way to optimize this information and speed up your success is to create your own Salon Success Team with two other salons. Have each salon owner / stylist invest in a copy of this book, and treat it like a book club – meet once a week and work through it, applying it and helping each other along the way.

Together, we can do amazing things. Don't see them as your competition, but rather as Collaborators.

Phase One
Foundation

You, First.

As the salon owner, you lead by example. You're always on time, you always dress well, your grooming is impeccable, you have a great, positive, optimistic attitude, you're reliable, committed, focused, disciplined, and excited about your business. You're realistic, too, and always looking for ways to improve and evolve yourself and your business. Your business is an extension of your philosophy; it's a reflection of who you are. You would no more have weeds growing in the grass in front of your salon than you would walk around with mud on your face, because, in a way, your salon IS your face.

You don't expect your employees to do what you won't do. In order to maintain your attitude and motivation, you watch your input: what you read and listen to and watch, where you go, whom you mix with, how you spend your time. You watch your health, exercise, and diet, and you're careful to remember that you are the driving force behind your business. No excuses. You take full responsibility.

Standardize, and Systematize

Since most of my readers won't hire me as their personal business coach or salon trainer to tailor these ideas and concepts to fit their particular salon in order to fast track their progress, it is important for you to make notes, keep records, and build a manual for your stylists and other employees to follow – just like a franchise handbook. By creating your own Systems Manual, you can be sure that things happen correctly every time, and that your employees, no matter how many salons you run and own, know exactly what to do.

When I trained high-end Carlton Hair International company-owned salons in South Africa and across the world in Orange County, California, every salon abode by the same guidelines and rules, hence their extraordinary success.

Understanding Incentives

People are different, and they require different motivation. We will discuss this later in this book. But generally speaking, you will do very well when you learn to incentivise every choice you wish people to make. Give them a good reason for taking every step along the way. People want to feel accepted, loved, important, and that their opinions matter. They want to feel special. They want to feel that they got a good deal, that the transaction is Win/Win, that the salon reciprocates their patronage, that there is a reward for their loyalty. Did you notice that this is all about the way you make people FEEL?

Remember: every step needs to offer a real reward. It has to be a system. Good systems work; that's why the MacDonald's system includes asking us, "Would you like fries with that?" every single time. You can't build a bridge without systems, nor can you build your salon business without systems. The ideas here have been tested in thousands of salons. They work if you use them correctly. We need to motivate our clients as well as our staff.

Incentives, compensation, and rewards are not all in the form of money. In fact, the best incentives have little to do with money and everything to do with the way you make your clients and employees feel. If you look at the Red Hat Society, you will learn a lot about what motivates people. This is a very successful organization. My beautiful wife of 27 years, Rika, is a Queen in one of the Red Hat groups, so I get a lot of exposure to this organization. She is a particularly good Queen and leader, so I learn well. More about motivation later.

Also remember that women are generally motivated by different things than men are, but ultimately, we all want to feel good. It's very important to know your target market demographic, so that your incentives can be crafted and honed to match your market. Is it predominantly male or female? Younger or older? What income range? White collar or blue collar? Retired or employed?

What works for one group could irritate, even offend another group. The environment in the salon – music, colours, pace, volume, should also all fit your ideal customer. For example, older people don't want too much noise or loud rap music. All clients want to feel their stylists can relate to them and their needs, so a stylist in her early twenties would be less successful with a client in her fifties than a stylist in a closer age bracket would.

USP (Unique Selling Proposition – What Makes Your Salon Special.)

How do you set yourself apart from your competition? How would you become the "Only Act in Town"? ADDED VALUE.

Most important, we should focus on the Relationship your staff have with clients, and their Experience in the salon: they may forget what you said, but they will remember how you made them feel.

Second, we should create systems that are predictable and effective. That's why you might prefer a franchised restaurant to a greasy spoon in a strange town; you know what to expect. And people feel secure when they know what is going to happen next. In this fast-changing, unpredictable, scary world, your salon should be a haven of peace and security where people are recognized, accepted, and liked.

I'll always remember when I had hair to cut (I'm bald now) and a stylist breathed out a disgusting stream of tobacco breath on me while I was captive in her chair. Now that poor stylist probably had no idea how offended I felt, or why. "Did I say something wrong?" Or when Rika came home from a salon experience and told me that the stylist was constantly looking at the door for new clients instead of focusing on Rika's hair.

This booklet is designed to help you to set yourself apart from your competition. Here are a few ideas to start with; a lot more to come!

Open the door for the client, when they arrive and when they leave - open their car door, give them an umbrella when it's raining – you can buy one for two dollars in a dollar store. Most salons would never think of doing that; they're simply "too busy."

Remember, people will pay $34,000 for a gold Rolex Presidential watch, when they can buy a cheap $15 watch that basically does the same job. Why? Scarcity – something special. How do you feel when you wear a Rolex? How do you feel when you wear a cheap watch? FEELINGS. We want people to see our watch – it makes us feel important and special, doesn't it?

Make a phone call for them, remember and use their names, attend a Dale Carnegie course – they're outstanding and they help improve our human relations. Reach right into their homes by using personalized Welcome Cards and Thank You cards, (I use the SendOut Cards service – highly recommended – let me know if you need a contact for that) that they can put on the mantelpiece and show their friends.

Do what other salons are too cheap, arrogant, or lazy to do. Do things they haven't even thought of. If your service is exceptional, you can NAME YOUR PRICE. But exceptional value has to come before increased prices. We have to chop the wood and make the fire before we can expect to get the heat, right?

Have you thought about issuing your clients with Preferred Client lapel pins? After all, multimillion dollar Network Marketing companies and training companies have proven over and over again how powerful lapel pin rewards are, and you can have different levels of pin – ruby, diamond – as rewards for referrals, long patronage, etc. Incentives.

Think about framed certificates, special invitations, acknowledgements, Customer Loyalty Events. Would you send your clients flowers on their birthdays or wedding anniversaries? What if you could send them GIFTS that DIDN'T COST YOU ANYTHING?

FREE? Did you say, "Free?"

Yup. Think about it. First, let's think about your salon. If ten people came into your hair salon for a free haircut on a quiet day and experienced your great service, how many of them would come back and become regular clients? Four? Well, that's four new clients that you wouldn't have had, and the cost was extremely low, wasn't it? A bit of hot water and a few chemicals. Low acquisition cost. And the better your service gets, the better the experience they enjoy in your salon, the more likely those clients will beg to come back!

What is the Lifetime Value of a Client?

Now, how much is a client really worth to you? For example, if a client spends just $40 per visit and comes into your salon every seven weeks on average, and if your average client stays with you for four years, that's a whopping $1,188.57!

And if we increase the average transaction value from $40 to $50 per visit, if we increase the frequency of their visits to every six weeks instead of seven, and if we can keep them for five years instead of four, their Lifetime Value jumps from $1,188.57 to $2,166!

And if that client, whom we wouldn't have had without offering them a free haircut, brings you JUST ONE new client by referring them to you, using one of the systems I will explain later, their value doubles to $4,333.33! Most salon owners never do these calculations or measure these numbers.

So how does this get you free stuff to give away? Well, doesn't the same concept of giving away the initial service at no charge apply to other services, like nail bars, spas, beauty salons, and so on? Of course it does. Once you explain this concept to the owner of a nearby nail bar and he or she understands and agrees to provide you with Gift Certificates for a free nail service – pedicure, manicure, polishing – valued at $50, you can GIVE AWAY free gifts valued at $50 each! And you can use these freebies as rewards for referrals or any other action you want to incentivise.

Chances are very good that your competition is not doing this. Get it in place and perfect it before they do!

"If you don't look good, we don't look good."
~ Vidal Sassoon

A Note on Gift Certificates:

Good quality paper, well designed, ideally in an envelope, and printed on it should be the exact service and the value of that service, plus the words, "With the Compliments of..." – that's where you write the name of your salon – plus "Subject to Availability" (you can slot these appointments in whenever you wish), "No Purchase Required," and "Not Transferable" – you could even write the name of the person receiving it on the Gift Certificate – this avoids people giving these Gift Certificates to homeless people, bums, or others who can't afford to buy the services under normal circumstances. Use both sides of the Gift Certificate to advertise your business, but realize this very important fact: Just handing these out doesn't work – people will think they're simply adverts. You have to tell people exactly what they're receiving; explain that is a free, no-obligation gift from your salon, and tell them WHY they are receiving it, so that you can reinforce what they are doing or initiate the things you want them to do.

Remember how Group Dynamics work: people tend to follow the crowd. They want to do what everyone else is doing. That's why we call them "sheeple." They want to belong to the "in crowd." If you go to a trade show, note how the people go to the booth where there are many other people. Crowds attract crowds. A busy salon attracts more clients.

We want what we can't have. That's why we want diamonds instead of river stones: perceived value and scarcity. We want to feel successful, wealthy, fit, attractive, noticed. Which brings me to the subject of your stylists.

Your Stylists Should Look Good.

They should dress well. They should, ideally, be in shape. They should speak well and not use bad language. "The better the hair of the stylist, the more money she makes." I'm sure you've experienced that. You saw what I wrote about the stylist that smoked earlier. More and more salons and businesses are refusing to hire smokers – smoke breaks, smelly breath (even when they chew gum to hide the odour) and clothes, bad health – many reasons. If you do have a stylist who smokes and he or she sincerely wants to stop, there are many aids available to do so. I have a friend who is an ex-smoker. She hypnotizes smokers who want to stop in 60 minutes and she has a 90% success rate. When your clients are served by good looking, well dressed professionals with great hair, they feel good. They feel respected. They will pay more for the service. Create an atmosphere of style and quality.

Adding Value

In addition to all the above ideas, why not create a Client Database and send out a weekly newsletter? I have done this for many years with a tremendous return on investment. Every week on the same day at the same time, people who subscribe to my free newsletter at www.LeverageAdvantage.com receive their newsletter. These newsletters are created to motivate, inform, and advertise. They set me apart as a specialist in the area of collaborative marketing. I use www.Aweber.com since I have found it to be the best and safest, and if you're worried about content, there is a mass of free, interesting information, articles, and motivational stuff on the Internet. Just be careful to acknowledge the writers. You're welcome to use any articles from my Blog, www. RobinJElliott.com, as long as you include my name and a link to my website.

You can also use your weekly newsletters to make people aware of new products, special events and offers, and recommended booklets, and of course to recommend or thank or reward people, especially your clients. When people see their names in your newsletter, many of them will forward it to their friends and family! If you don't have the time to do your newsletter, use a Virtual Assistant. It's a great little investment with a big ROI (return on investment) if done properly.

Of course, using Social Media works, too – I recommend a Facebook Fan Page and LinkedIn only. You can also use this medium to reward and congratulate your clients, and they will share those posts with their friends and connections.

Rika (She Who is Amazing) and I were in a mall and she bought something. When she opened the bag when we got home, she discovered a chocolate in the bag with her purchase. She called the store and they responded that they include a chocolate in every bag. Such a small cost and such a big impact! You can buy small chocolates, but please stick to good quality chocolate.

How would you feel if your stylist called you up and said, "Sally, as a thank you gesture for your patronage of / referrals to Inter Hair Design, I have been authorized to present you with a gift with our gratitude and compliments, valued at $50." (Gift Certificate for a free facial, pedicure, massage – that you don't pay for.) And perhaps Sally receives the Gift Certificate when she comes in for her next haircut. That might just speed up her next visit...

Do you provide FOOD or BEVERAGES to your clients? How about their guests? We have even provided MENUS so clients could choose what they would like to eat – on the house / no charge. A cup of good coffee will cost you around 25 cents.

New Clients

People remember two things: First and Last Impressions. (Remember? Last Impressions are Lasting Impressions.) They remember their first visit to your salon. You only get one chance at a first impression.

One of the ways to make absolutely sure that we make a good impression on new clients is to have the receptionist attach a small pink sticker to the back of the cape they wear to protect their clothes. Anyone passing behind them can see the sticker. When employees see the sticker, they should be trained to greet the new client in a friendly and professional, not a gushing, false manner. "Hi, you're new to our salon. Welcome! My name is Johnny, and I look forward to being of service to you. And what is your name, Madam / Sir?" Note the Madam or Sir address. This, alone, sets you worlds apart from the competition. Only "Call me Antoinette" should be allowed to reduce this to first name terms.

Client Files

Every client should have a client file in which details of the work done, chemicals used, dates of visits, transaction amounts (spend per visit), plus personal information, is noted. If this is good enough for successful giants like Ritz Carlton, it should work for us.

Imagine, for instance, that client Betty tells the stylist that her son's ninth birthday is coming up, and the salon sends him a personalized card with a picture of him on the front (grabbed from Facebook). With SendOut Cards, it's very affordable. Or that she mentioned that she was worried about her husband going to hospital. Next visit, the stylist reads her file before greeting her, and then, when the stylist sees her, says, "And tell me, Betty, how is Fred doing?" Wow!

What if you find out that client Anne's Hot Button (what she really, really loves) is knitting, and the stylist buys her a magazine of knitting patterns before her next visit? You'll OWN her. You can see a multitude of ways we can use this information to create a massively personal and valued relationship with your clients – huge reciprocity.

Client files can create miracles if used correctly, and the information can be used to help with your statistics. More about stats and measurement later in this book.

Quick thought: Grab your iPad and allow the client to sign up for your Salon Newsletter while she's in the salon, and she receives an additional Gift Certificate (different to the one she has already received.)

"I always wanted to be a hairdresser." ~ David Beckham

Motivating Employees:
Intrinsic vs Extrinsic Motivation

The old model that was used to motivate people was carrot and stick - reward and punishment - extrinsic motivation. That is fast becoming replaced with Intrinsic Motivation – what people will do without external inducement. Intrinsically motivating activities are those in which people will engage for no reward other than the interest and enjoyment that accompanies them. For example, people will play in orchestras for no remuneration.

As long as their needs are fulfilled, we can use the power of intrinsic motivation to have our employees perform very well indeed. At some point, it's no longer about the money. Donald Trump, for example, doesn't need the money – he loves making money - it is a hobby for him, a game, a challenge – he is intrinsically motivated. And we don't have to be as rich as Trump to be intrinsically motivated. You don't have to pay me to ride my bike.

As long as people are receiving fair salaries and their needs are met and they are comfortable and secure, three things have to be in place in order for intrinsic motivation to work very well:

1. Autonomy – provide your employees with autonomy over some (or all) of the four main aspects of work: When they do it, how they do it, whom they do it with (the team and the people they serve) and what they do (don't ask me to do admin!)

2. Mastery – allow your staff to become better at something that matters to them: not too difficult or too easy – some challenge involved, and a workplace that makes it possible for them to learn and master their work with goals, feedback, and some freedom (autonomy.)

3. Purpose – create a workplace where they can contribute to a greater cause. Communicate it. They should understand the purpose and mission of your business, not just the money goals. "To help women feel beautiful and thus enhance every aspect of their lives: their relationships, self-esteem, parenting, level of achievement..." that sort of thing. This should be as important as making money in the salon. Everyone should "buy in" to this purpose in their own way, so use words like "we" and "us."

Daniel H. Pink's book, "DRIVE," will help you understand this better.

Motivation That Costs Very Little:

It is vitally important to know your people. What drives them, what keeps them awake at night, what are their goals? What is their "Hot Button" – in other words, what do they really, really want? A trip to Hawaii with their partner? A spa treatment? A college education for their child? A new car? New clothes? More friends? Security? As a leader, you need to know their family, their problems and aspirations, fears, hopes and dreams.

Some powerful motivational actions cost very little: a pat on the back, a kind word, a genuine interest in their personal concerns, a phone call, a meal with them, a Thank You card. When we understand people, we can make small things count a lot, like a surgeon who knows just where to cut, a musician that knows how to make beautiful music come out of an old instrument. Every employee is an instrument; good leaders know how to play them to make amazing music that everyone enjoys. Sending a bunch of flowers at exactly the right time can be more effective than a $500 check.

"A hair in the head is worth two in the brush."
~ Oliver Herford

Personality Types (DiSC)

A client of mine who owned a hair salon in California radically improved his business when we tested his employees to establish their personality styles and re-organized the business. We all have characteristics of all the four major personality styles, however one is normally dominant. In business, it's important to acknowledge our strengths and leverage them, and to find others to supplement our weaknesses. There's no right or wrong character type. Here's a quick overview.

The High D – Dominant style (minority of people, hardest to find) is bottom-line and results oriented, impatient, sometimes tactless, driven and extroverted, with weaknesses in details. Major fear: being taken advantage of / ripped off. Major need: Control. Freedom. Good closers, great pioneers.

The High I – Influencing style is an extrovert, "party animal", great at meeting people and starting relationships, popular, good opener, weakness is details and time management. Major fear: being embarrassed in public. Major need: Looking good to others. Being liked and accepted.

The High C – Cautious style is introverted, loves details, numbers and systems more than people, excellent numbers people and accountants, computer experts, analysts. Weakness is over analysis; fear is criticism of their work. Highly analytical. Major need: Details.

The High S – Steady style (70% - majority of people) is an introvert, loyal, team player, family type, great systems and support person, needs security and long term relationships, fears risk, conflict and change, especially unexpected change. Needs others to make things happen and to create change and to take unpopular action when necessary. Major fear: Unexpected change. Major need: Security.

This is a simplistic approach, but understanding our strengths and weaknesses and allowing people to do what they're good at, while avoiding tasks that they're weak at, is simply smart business sense. For technical sales we use High C's and S's. Ideal sales-people are normally High D's with secondary I's. One wouldn't want an accountant who is a High D, or a High S to launch a new business. You don't want a High C to be the host at a cocktail party and we don't want two High I's behind a reception desk because they'll talk all day! Sometimes, the D's will fight each other for control, so they need different areas to control.

Using personality style analysis has helped many of my clients to be better entrepreneurs and leaders and to hire the appropriate people. Self knowledge is essential to success. I use the DiSC style analysis – there are many others available, but I like this one. When training teams and employees, I use DiSC to build understanding and relationships.

Selling to High D's: Talk results and ROI and close early and hard.

Selling to High I's: Build relationship, have fun and close early.

Selling to High C's: Provide copious details and proof and take time to close.

Selling to High S's: Prove that the support and relationships will be in place long after the sale is made and close slowly.

Managing High D's: Give them lots of control and clear objectives and do what you say you will do.

Managing High I's: Reward them publicly, make them look good and watch their time allocation.

Managing High C's: Be specific, don't rush them, and compliment their work (catch them doing some
thing right), set time goals.

Managing High S's: Make changes slowly, provide lots of
security, share long-term plans.

Naturally, this DiSC model applies to our vendors and clients, too.
If you're interested in having your team tested, let me know.

A Few Important Points:

- Do you have a mobile friendly website for your salon?
- Is your website up to date with up to date testimonials from cli-
ents? (Use the real, full names of clients; not "A.G. in Atlanta.")
- Do you use video as much as possible on your website?
- Have you considered text marketing?

NOW, we are finally ready to start on the next three Phases of
doubling your salon profits!

We have handled the foundation, and we're ready to jump in to
the building. Like any skyscraper, the foundation is very important. The fact that this booklet is designed to help you double
your profits doesn't mean you have to stop there. You can keep
on growing your profits as long as you like with the magical Back
End, which we will discuss in Phase Four.

"Long, beautiful, gleaming, streaming, flaxen, waxen...
I adore hair!"
~James Rado and Gerome Ragni, Hair

Phase Two
All About SALES: Fill Your Chairs with the Right People

Hair Shows

My salon owner clients have been very successful with many of the systems I have crafted, and one of them is the Hair Show. Ideally, as with all my clients in every industry, there should be no cost and no risk to my client to implement these systems. The Hair Show is no exception.

First, it's best to use your salon for the venue. If the salon is too small, find an appropriate venue as close to the salon as possible. The nicer the salon and the venue, of course, the higher quality client you can attract.

How do you pay for a venue if you're not using your salon? Ask the hair product companies you use to sponsor the venue and to provide you with samples, gift baskets, and door prizes. You may find that one of them will do this if you agree to allow them to be the only product company sponsoring and if you allow their sales rep to attend the show. No problem, if they provide what you want. And you're not confined to using hair product companies as sponsors, of course; include anyone who would like access to those attending, e.g. financial planners, Realtors, mortgage brokers, interior designers.

The objective of the hair show is to get new clients. We want to make a great impression on our visitors and sign them up, so most of the attendees should be prospective clients, not existing clients.

How do you find people to attend? First, by now you know your target market. Look at your client list.

Now look for three clients that:

1. Represent your target market
2. Have really great hair
3. Are loyal, regular clients
4. Will give you a testimonial at the hair show
5. Are Centres of Influence (she knows, influences and communicates with a lot of people in your target market.)

Ask her if she will help you to promote your Hair Show and be your Diplomat. If she is a Hair Show Diplomat, she has the responsibility of inviting people to attend and to be there to give a testimonial. In return, you will do her hair that afternoon at no cost and she will look fantastic! If you have photos of these clients before they got their hair fixed by you, you can project a BEFORE picture of them on the screen before they emerge as one of your hair show models! (Before and After effect.)

These Diplomats (Centres of Influence) can hand out tickets to the show as well, but they need to know exactly what kind of clients you're looking for – age, income, gender, etc. Tickets should note that they have to book a seat since seating is limited, and that attendees will receive prizes, food and beverages and a great, educational show. There will also be networking and socializing before the event (especially if you're targeting businesswomen).

Food, water, teas, juices, and coffees can be donated by local caterers or restaurants in return for their names on the tickets and their fliers in the "Goodie Bag" that each attendee receives.

Each attendee should receive their Goodie Bag with their gifts when they arrive and register. You want their name, telephone number, and email address. Then they get the Goodie Bag, then they get their seat.

Then there is socializing and networking, and there can be more socializing and networking after the show, but keep it short; the focus is the hair show, not networking. And your sponsors should not be allowed to "hard sell."

You (the salon owner) are the Master of Ceremonies, and you welcome the people, thank your sponsors, and let everyone know that there will be a special Big Gift going to one lucky person at the end of the show. Tell them what the Big Gift is. Tell them about your salon, introduce and compliment each of your staff and stylists by name, and establish the expectations: "Our clients come back every 6 weeks because they are a walking advertisement for this salon – we want them to look great at all times, and that means we need to see them every six weeks. And they use the products we recommend, not cheap knock-offs from wholesalers..." This is very important.

Now you run your show, each model appearing after you've shown her "Before" picture on the screen (you can team up with nail bars, beauty salons, and clothing boutiques if you like – more about this in Phase Four – in which case the models look spectacular.)

At the end of the show, you have a very exciting, Big Announcement: "I know you've all been waiting, hoping you'll be the lucky one to win the Big Prize (tell them again what the Big Prize consists of – and it can include Gift Certificates from the sponsoring Nail Bar, Spa, and so on, and of course products) – well, I have wonderful news – every one of you that was impressed with the show tonight that makes an appointment with us for your hair will receive a Big Prize!" Your employees and sponsors have been told to clap and applaud loudly at this point.

Now your receptionist goes around making appointments. If someone says they have to check their diary at home, tell them they have until 12 noon the next day to make their appointment in order to receive their Big Prize. If someone doesn't wish to make an appointment, don't make a big deal out of it, don't embarrass them. Don't brush them off. Smile, be friendly. "Hey, no problem, Wanda. When you're ready, you know where to find us. "No" simply means "I'm not ready YET."

NOW HERE is a very important point: When do those who set up their appointments with you get their Big Prizes? When they leave after their appointment. Not before, or many of them will simply cancel their appointment and run off with their Big Prize, giggling. I know. We have done many of these hair shows.

If you get appointments with 50% of the women, and they're all impressed, you've done well. Remember the Lifetime Value of a client? And the show didn't cost you anything! You can do Hair shows regularly. It's a great way to get more clients.

How can you get every attendee of your hair show to sign up online for your newsletter? Offer to send them a free Gift Certificate (from another business) in the mail when they sign up online. You should always be encouraging everyone to sign up for your newsletter. Use Social Media to do that, too. Ask your Facebook friends and LinkedIn connections to SHARE the offer on their social media – "Sign up for this great newsletter and receive ..."

"Hairdressing in general hasn't been given the kudos it deserves. It's not recognized by enough people as a worthy craft."
~ Vidal Sassoon

Gift Certificates

We have already discussed the power of Gift Certificates. By targeting people you want as clients and providing them with a Gift

Certificate for a free haircut, no cost, no obligation, and you do a great job, and if their experience is outstanding, some of them will become regular clients. Be sure to include "Not Transferable" on the certificates and insert the name of the person being given the Gift Certificate. Also, "Only One Use Per Person" so they don't keep coming back with another Gift Certificate.

This way, you fill empty chairs during quiet times and days, and nobody will know they didn't pay. The more people in the salon, the more paying clients you will attract. It's human nature. One night, Rika and I drove past a restaurant that always has a line-up out of the door and down the sidewalk. Rika said, "They must have great food!" See? She might even have suggested we try the restaurant, but she knows I won't stand in a line. Just handing out Gift Certificates won't work – the person presenting it must explain what they're gifting them with.

You can fill all your vacant chairs continuously with freebies from your Gift Certificates, especially if you have other people distributing them for you. The better your service, the higher the percentage of freebies that will become loyal, paying clients. It's very important to give these gift certificates to the right prospective clients in the right way. If you're committed to this, you can have all the chairs filled, continuously, within a week or two. I have seen this done many times. Explain to your employees how it works before you start. They should afford the freebies the same level of excellent service as they do paying clients.

Cross Promotion

When you have your newsletter working, you can use it for cross promotions. If you have a friend whose business targets the same people that you do, suggest to them the following: "Why don't we do a cross promotion for three weeks? I'll promote your business and you promote mine. I could put your fliers / business cards in my salon, promote you in my newsletter. How could you promote me?"

It is very important to get this agreement in writing, so nobody forgets what they promised to do. It's not a complicated legal contract. It's just, "Belinda agrees to..... from March 1 to April 1 and Ron agrees to.... for the same period." It is also very important to measure the results of this joint venture. See Phase Three about how to do that.

It is equally important that you both DO what you agree to do, in the way you agree to do it. For example, if Ron has agreed that he will feature you in his newsletter for three weeks, sign up for his newsletter, give him the script and pictures he needs, and check every week that he does it. If he agrees to put your fliers in his offices, check. He might just have "forgotten."

Events

If there are big events in your neighbourhood and your ideal audience is there, offer to be a sponsor – donate a door prize (yes, it's a Gift Certificate for a free haircut) – and you get exposure to the entire group from the front of the room. Only sponsor when there is no cost or risk to you. Let your product vendors donate door prizes, too. The other night I attended a Chamber of Commerce event and gave the President one of my books to hand out as a Door Prize. She responded they already had enough door prizes for that night, but that she would be grateful if she could use it as a door prize at their AGM. That means that I will be promoted (via the book door prize announcement) at an event that I'm not even attending. That's great leverage, isn't it?

"Those curious locks so aptly twin'd,
Whose every hair a soul doth bind."
~Thomas Carew

Barter

I don't suggest you use services like GroupOn. They attract "cheapies" who have no money or who are tightwads. Check out www.tradeexchangecanada.ca to learn how you can use trade / barter to leverage your excess capacity (empty chairs) and earn trade / barter dollars that you can use to buy things you would normally spend cash on, like printing, signage, design, printer cartridges – almost any services you can think of. I have used barter dollars for 13 years and I never had a trade dollar I couldn't spend. You make the rules, for example, "we only accept trade on the first visit to our salon. After that, it's cash." (I've also never met a Dollar I didn't like.)

Joining a trade / barter company also gets you massive exposure, and it's a great investment if used correctly. The trade company will give you a trade manual. Read it. Ask questions, work with your broker. Before you spend cash on something, ask if it's available on trade. Many of the trade companies are linked, even internationally, so the scope is amazing. It's well worth taking a good look at.

"Hair style is the final tip-off whether or not a woman really knows herself."
~Hubert de Givenchy,Vogue, July 1985

Contingency Advertising

We all know how risky and expensive advertising is, and how seldom it works. If you track the results of your advertising, test, measure, tweak, and improve it, some ads work very well, but it's still very much like gambling. When it doesn't work, the advertising rep rubs his greasy hands together and says, "You need a bigger ad! You haven't been advertising for long enough! Give me more money!"

OK. Some ads do work, and it does get your name out there, but how can you advertise with NO RISK? Here's what you can do. It doesn't work with every advertiser, but I've used it and my clients have used it very successfully over the years. When the sales rep drops in and pitches you, get in touch with the manager or owner. The sales rep can't do this; he usually doesn't understand it and all he wants is commissions.

This is the way it works. First, you have to know what the Lifetime Value is of one of your clients – your average client. Let's assume it's $2,000. How much would you pay for $2,000? How much would you pay to buy a client? That's what most "coaches" would ask you. And that can get you into trouble, because it could really hurt your cash flow. MY suggestion is, never pay more for a client than they spend on their first visit. Remember that, and stay safe. The fact that I am risk averse has kept me in business for a long time.

OK, here we go. The advertiser wants $300 for the advert. You ask him, "If you were me, and you placed this $300 ad, I know you can only guess, but how many clients would you expect from this $300 advert? Twenty? I need enough clients to justify this ad!"

The advertiser responds, "Well, I can't promise anything (always covering his a$$) but I think yes, 20 clients would be reasonable."

YOU: "So you think it's reasonable that I could expect to get about 20 clients from this ad, but of course you can't guarantee that. OK. How about I pay you DOUBLE for this advert? $600? Would you like that?"

ADVERTISER: "Of course! But why would you do that?"

YOU: "Easily. You place the ad. All responses go direct to you, so you have full control. You send me the names of the respondents, I invite them into my salon, and I pay you $30 for every new client. 20 new clients = $600. I can't guarantee that, but based on what you said, it's a good deal. The ad doesn't cost you anything - you have the space. And you control the names, so there's no risk to you if the ad doesn't work. I pay you contingent on results. If I only get half of the predicted 20 clients, you still get your $300!

This has worked for me and my clients with radio, TV, print magazines, newspapers, signage, you name it. Many advertisers won't do it, but some do. After all, they have the space, and if they're using up dead space, there's no risk to them or to you. And if the ads don't pull, you still get a lot of exposure and branding and the ad space is full – you both look good and you haven't lost a cent.

Try it. If you ask enough advertisers, you'll get a few. "Some will, some won't, so what? Next!" You have to kiss the frogs to find the princes.

"The hair is the richest ornament of women."
~ Martin Luther

Hair Celebrities

In North America, people love and worship celebrities. Perhaps we actually believe what we see in the movies and that's why we think movie stars are so smart and brave. Anyway, people emulate, copy, adore celebrities – buy the same clothes, and so on. And in a big company, the top management are celebrities to those under them. They like to copy their bosses.

Many years ago in South Africa, there was a very successful chain of coffee shops called House of Coffees. I haven't seen their equal in quality in Canada. The owner and founder told me how he built his business. At that time, the average South African was drinking instant coffee. He wanted to educate us about real, delicious, brewed coffee. So he went to all the top executives in the banks and big corporations in our city, and gave them Gift Certificates for FREE COFFEE in his coffee shops for six months.

Once they started drinking his wonderful coffee, they got hooked on it. They became regular customers. And all their underlings followed their bosses into the House of Coffees, cowering in the corners, hoping that the bosses would notice them. After all, that's where the top brass went! And that is how he built his business. No advertisements, no fliers, no banners. Just celebrity coffee.

Let's apply that to your celebrities – Celebrity Hair. Test it, and see if it works for you. One important thing – the agreement with them has to be that:

1. While they use your salon, they don't use any other salon, and
2. You can advertise the fact that they use your service.

If you provide all your clients with Preferred Client lapel pins, you can also ask your Hair Celebrities to wear them, too. Here's the thing: if the lapel pins look cheap and gaudy and too big, your clients won't wear them. They'll put them on when they arrive at your salon and take them off as soon as they leave your salon. I used to issue my Mentor Clients (they each paid me $20,000 for one week on training) a small, solid gold dollar sign lapel pin like the one I sometimes wear. Guess what? People begged me for one of those pins. I had a jeweler friend of mine make them for me by hand, and they only cost me $50 each at the time. Small, discreet, beautiful, high quality jewelry is valued. And if people don't know what they mean, they'll ask – an even more effective way to promote the salon! "What is that little gold sign you have on your lapel, Angelina Jolie?" "Oh, that's the hair salon I use!" "What? Where is that salon? What's it called? It must be great if Angelina uses it! What's their number?"

Referrals from Your Clients

NOTE: A "Referral" means someone is referred to your salon by a client and they come and pay for their service and products – not a Gift Certificate or a freebie. Also, they've never been to your salon before, not even the Hair Show.

Yes, this is the best one, but it has to be systematized. Haphazardly asking clients to refer you to their friends for no reward seldom works. That's called the Shotgun Approach, as opposed to a high powered sniper rifle. I have found the best way to do this is to offer individual rewards, as well as The Big Prize for the Most Referrals. In that way, the client who refers only one new client gets rewarded, and the client who refers many new clients gets rewarded for each one, and the one who refers the most gets rewarded for each one PLUS he or she wins the Big Prize. Rewards should be donated by other businesses, not paid for, and you can use Trade Dollars to buy great prizes, too. Of course you're welcome to pay if you like, but the cost of the reward per referral should never be more than the average client spends in one visit. That's the safe way to do it.

Rewards can be accumulated, as well. This is VERY powerful, especially if the referring client is a big Centre of Influence. Let's say the client tells you she wants $500 to buy a particular thing. You could say, "Well, Bessie, how about this? Get our Layaway Program! The way it works is simple: For every referral you bring us, we credit your account with $30. When it gets to $500, I write you a check for $500!" That means that Bessie will be "locked in" - committed - to bringing you referrals until she hits $500.

"A woman who cuts her hair is about to change her life."
~ Coco Chanel

WHY, for Most Men, Gifts are a Stronger Incentive Than Money

Visit any mall and notice that most of the stores are aimed at women shoppers. See the bored boyfriends and husbands lurking and lounging and wishing the eternal day of shopping would end so they can go home and watch sports? Women receive diamond engagement rings, men get nothing. Women get gifts for Valentines Day, men usually get nothing. Women spend a fortune on wedding dresses – men simply put on a suit. Most of them would avoid the expensive wedding if they could. In the U.S., women oversee 80% of consumer spending, totalling $3.7 trillion. They control more than $20 trillion or about 70% of global consumer spending. Women are responsible for 85% of consumer purchases. On average, women spend 8 hours shopping per month.

What am I saying? Men work hard to earn money, women work hard to earn it AND to spend it. Sure, they work hard; nothing is harder than raising kids and running a home, and fewer and fewer North American women stay home to raise the kids – most raise kids AND have a job. Women influence 91% of home sales. They buy much, much more stuff than men, and they get most of the presents. Men get very few gifts compared to women, and in North America, frankly (I'm known for not pulling my punches), men are whipped. The women run the money and most men need permission to buy themselves the toys they so dearly want.

This is important information for those who wish to incentivise the actions of male customers, salespeople, affiliates, employees, and joint venture partners. For customer loyalty and retention, to increase transaction value, and to encourage referrals, think TOYS and FUN for men. The fact is, you can achieve a lot more using gifts than money to motivate men. Mommy won't let him buy another set of golf clubs, since he hardly uses the ones he's got. She doesn't think he needs the latest toys and gadgets more than the kids need new clothes, and money is better spent paying down family debt than a new gun / knife / iPad / kayak / skis / rims for his truck. She may be right, but Daddy wants that bigger screen TV very badly, and he's prepared to work for it.

Getting down to incentives, Mommy can't complain and it's not Daddy's fault that he was given a beautiful new radial arm saw by his sales manager when he was the top area salesperson for December. Or that he won a brand new snowmobile for selling the most houses last year. He doesn't have to explain, argue, make excuses, or bargain. He has a way of getting all the fun things he wants by simply producing – more sales, more referrals, more whatever you want him to do. And often the toys you buy men cost less than the commissions you would have paid, especially if your company sells the stuff.

In addition, the motivation for gadgets and toys is usually a lot higher and more intense than earning more money to pay for boring, mundane things like makeup and food and debt and mortgages and clothes (women's clothes) and facials and manicures and the hairdresser and handbags… When is the last time you heard a man shout, "Oh, boy! I can't wait to work through the night to win the sales competition so my wife can get that new outfit and impress her friends!" or "I will do whatever it takes to make this deal so that we can pay down the mortgage two years sooner!" But he could get extremely animated and highly enthusiastic about a fishing trip. And often, the scoundrels won't report the gifts on their tax returns…

In my own business, I once helped a client sell all his franchises out in three months (he hadn't sold one in a year) by adding an overseas trip "for training" – and having the new franchisee pay for it by increasing the price. Suddenly, the investors could justify an overseas holiday and make it tax deductible.

Personalizing incentives for men is equally important. We don't, thank Zeus, all get excited about golf, so don't assume we do. For one man it's electronic toys, for another it's guns, and for someone else it may be a certain brand of single malt scotch. A carefully researched, chosen, and matched incentive, offered in the correct way, can create a massive ROI.

Reactivate Past Clients

Make up a list of your clients who haven't visited your salon for five months or more. Call them up, or have someone call them for you. At one point they were customers, so they know you and there might be a good reason why they're not in the salon.

"Hello, Vivian? I'm Roberto, and I'm calling from Salon Hair Fair. You're a valued client of ours, and we notice you were last here visiting us in February. Is everything OK with you? (Answer the question, deal with complaints, listen carefully.) You know, Vivian, we prefer to serve known friends than unknown strangers, and we'd love to have you back. So [Salon Owner's Name] has arranged a Welcome Home Gift Package for all Returning Friends valued at $300! Yes, if you come in for any service before the end of the month, we will present you with your Welcome Home Package. Let me tell you what it consists of. [these are Gift Certificates from other businesses at no cost to you] – Two free tennis lessons valued at $90, a facial worth $60, a manicure or pedicure valued at $50, a free Tae Kwondo class valued at... When can I make your appointment for, Vivian?"

Practice the script so that it sounds natural, be enthusiastic, but allow the client to talk and listen carefully. This can bring a lot of clients back and help you fill your chairs!

"It's an ill will that blows when you leave the hairdresser."
~ Phyllis Diller

Finally, an Important Note on Networking

Every salon owner knows it's important to get out there and meet people, so I'm sure you're often out and about networking. When you factor in the cost of your most valuable and irreplaceable resource, your Time, it costs a lot of money to attend meetings – service clubs, networking meetings, events. Plus the hard costs: membership, entry fees, fines, plus gas, food, beverages, parking, car maintenance, transport, and so on. As a business owner, you should be calculating your return on that investment, and working on improving it.

When I attend an event and come away with a contact who is looking for a certain service or product, I expect to earn a decent commission when I connect them with the source of that product or service. That improves my ROI. It cost me a lot of money (time factored in) to attend the event and get the lead for Joe the plumber, so I expect to enjoy a piece of the profit he makes when he sells my referral a new sink.

We know that like attracts like, and birds of the feather flock together. If I attend events that are populated with a legion of losers – broke, self-employed salespeople – I'm not likely to turbo boost my ROI. On the other hand, if I pay to break bread with a huddle of heroes, a pack of producers, my ROI will skyrocket accordingly. Not only will the clustersuck of wanna-be's bore and frustrate me, but I will learn nothing and leave drained and angry, while that muster of masters will have me emerge motivated and inspired and I will learn a lot. So avoid the mass of misery and the deluge of the dumb and mix with the champions – the top dogs, not the mangy mongrels. Losers won't refer you to your best clients.

Living in a large city, I am grateful to have a lot of options when it comes to choosing where to spend my time. When I attended the talk by the minister of finance after Budget Day, I rubbed shoulders with CEO's and even an Honorary Consul at my lunch table, and I enjoyed the event immensely. $198 per ticket. Next week, I look forward to the Art of Leadership event – $398 per ticket – I expect to make some good connections there, too. In between, I attend other events of varying levels, and when I find myself in the middle of a puling parcel of parasites, I leave – fast. No ROI there.

Good people can introduce you to good people, so it's important to build on the good ones and remove the bad ones. Invest in relationships with good people, divest yourself of the also-rans. Give to get. When you sow to the wind, you will reap from the whirlwind. What goes around comes around. Investing your valuable time and skills in a flock of fools is just, well… foolish.

When you're at an event, you know that "talking in the interests of the other person and building the relationship before trying to do business" is very important, and winners automatically do this. When you meet with someone who is hell bent on selling you something and obviously isn't interested in you, you know you're talking to the wrong person. Withdraw from that conversation as fast as possible and look for a winner.

Finally, it's impossible to measure your ROI during or even soon after an event – some reaping will take place weeks, months, even years after you made the contact – but it is definitely possible to become selective where and with whom you spend your time. I know you sometimes find a diamond in the sewage, but not often enough, in my opinion, to warrant regular prospecting in poo. Respect yourself and your time. Ask yourself, "Who would a highly paid lawyer or accountant spend his time talking with?"

Next time you're circulating and percolating, moving and grooving, making the contacts and writing the contracts, remember this advice: Be the poorest and most unsuccessful person in the room, and your game will improve. Play with those who are poorer and less successful than you are, and... Seek out the leaders, the Centres of Influence, the rainmakers, and pay the price. It's worth every cent and every minute.

Phase Three

Measure Everything. Make sure it works, and make it work better!

Imagine if you discovered that a tenth of your day was absolutely wasted – every day. Or that what you thought was making you money was actually costing you money. Or that by replacing one activity with another, you could double the output. It's not as far fetched as it might sound. The cumulative effect and ripple effect of our choices can be very rewarding – or devastating.

Why don't we measure all activities, expenditures, use of resources, and options? Is it simply because it's easy NOT to? Because we're used to doing what we're doing? Our comfort zone? Avoidance of change? Our fragile egos? Scared of disturbing or upsetting the status quo? We "don't have the time?" We're not motivated? We discard or put off what is important in favour of what is urgent? Or is it simply that we don't know where to start?

Imagine a tennis player who divided his game into 10 contributing parts or activities, from his serve through his backhand, and worked on measuring and improving every single one of those components? If he improved each by an average of just 5%, he would see an overall improvement of a massive 50%! Here's the problem, though: You can't think out of the box while you're in it. And you can't learn from someone more screwed up than you are, weaker than you are, or less successful than you are. I help my clients measure every aspect of their business, including the activities of every employee, if they have employees, and we use strategies and techniques from other industries as well. We measure every 15 minutes – there's a form for that – and we look at alternatives. "Out of the box" implies an unthreatened, objective, open-minded, positive and flexible approach. We move our focus from sales to profits, and we recognize that testing and then implementing SYSTEMS as opposed to a haphazard, spray and pray, shotgun approach is essential for lasting success. Very few salon owners measure things the way they should.

Learn from MacDonalds, who found that the simple question, "Would you like fries with that?" can lose the company millions when ignored or the wrong words are used. The actual words, body language, presentation, timing, and leverage of each action should be considered. I am often amazed to find that businesses don't properly measure their sales ratios (leads, calls to those leads, reaching the prospect, getting appointments, actually seeing the prospect, closing, getting the sale, the referrals gleaned from each sale, and the back end value, or a variation based on the type of business), so they can't manage what they don't measure.

One of my clients improved his bottom line significantly by simply installing fake video cameras – it can be that simple.

The discovery process / measurement can be implemented easily and relatively quickly, and changes that include the correct leverage can be implemented without fuss. It's all in the way it's analyzed and done. My point is, without change, we are subject to entropy, and our competition may be smart enough to use innovation and change enough to put us out of business. On the other hand, we can leave our competition in our dust and grow faster than we thought with an inclusive, collaborative, analytical approach to business. This applies both to one-chair salons and multimillion dollar salon chains.

Measurement is essential to success in business. Think about that the next time you check the gas gauge in your car or pump the tires. Or read your bank balance. If you can't measure it, you can't manage it. You can't improve your profits. You can't tweak, adjust, or fix anything unless it is correctly measured.

Let's start with your existing situation and improve on it.

Time

Your time is your most valuable, irreplaceable resource. Top business owners know that "You should only do what only you can do – delegate everything else. Do what makes you the most money and gets you the best results. Start with measuring, for example, how you spend your valuable time every day. Draw up a chart that divides your day into fifteen minute segments on the horizontal lines, and then divide the day with ten vertical columns, each representing a different activity. Colour in one fifteen minute block every fifteen minutes, and at the end of the day, simply add up how much time, in total, you spent on each activity. Most salon owners find they spend too much time on the phone, too much time talking to people who can't help their business or bring them customers, and too much time on unproductive activities or even destructive activities.

Whatever you're doing during the day, stop and ask yourself, "Is what I am doing now taking me towards my goal or away from it? Is it making me more successful or less successful? What is the return on this time investment?" For example, I have clients who tell me they belong to fraternal clubs or Chambers of Commerce or Networking Clubs or Service Clubs because they think it will help their business. When we work out the amount of time and money they spend, and the dollar value of their time, and then we measure how much money this large investment has made them, however, they're losing money all the way to the bank. They make much more money when they resign from the club and replace that activity with one that is more productive. What else COULD you spend this time on? What are your alternatives? You're never going to get that time back! Learn to say NO. Learn to end the phone calls. Use Call Display. Learn to resign from organizations that are using you, taking advantage of you, and not worth your time. You can "Give Back" to society by writing a check if you like. Money is replaceable, but not your time. If you don't measure this stuff, you might never realize this.

"We learned to put discipline in the haircuts by using actual geometry, actual architectural shapes and bone structure. The cut had to be perfect and layered beautifully, so that when a woman shook it, it just fell back in." ~ Vidal Sassoon

Where Do Your New Clients Come From?

We should know where every new client comes from, who gave out every Gift Certificate that gets a prospective client in the door. If you don't know that, how would you know which of your advertisements is working, and which isn't? You should stop running ads that don't work instead of blindly buying more of them. 80/20: which 20% of your clients are bringing you 80% of your revenue?

You can get a far better return on your money when you pay for RESULTS (i.e. Rewards and commissions) than when you pay for PROMISES i.e. advertising and "sales reps" or "PR people." Do you spend a lot of time on social media? Fine. How much money is that making you? I measured this and immediately closed my Facebook account and my Facebook Fan Page. I left a fraternal club and a service club, two Chambers of Commerce and two networking clubs. I literally have better ways to spend my time and money. See? I actually practice what I preach.

"I think the most important thing a woman can have - next to talent, of course - is her hairdresser."
~ Joan Crawford

Let's Measure Your Statistics:

Out of every ten people who show up to take advantage of a Gift Certificate Free Haircut and Blow Dry, how many become paying clients? Three? How can we make our service so spectacular that we can increase that number to four and then five and then six?

What is the Lifetime Value of your clients right now? How much is the average bill, how many times per year do they come into the salon, and how many years do they last? We've discussed this before, but have you measured it in your salon? How can we improve these numbers? How many referrals do you get from your average client? How can we improve that number?

Break down what your customers spend with you – services, products – keep track of it all, and see how to improve each one. Talk with your product suppliers. Can you improve the sales techniques of your stylists? Do they need training? More training? Regular training? What kind of training?

Do you get feedback / appraisals from every client at the end of every visit? Do you measure that? Are you aware of the individual performance of each stylist? Do they need training in human relationships?

We want more clients, spending more money per transaction, coming back more often, staying with the salon longer, and bringing us more referrals. We want to convert more freebies into paying clients. We only want to spend money and time when we get a good return on that investment.

What would happen if you stayed open an hour later, or closed an hour earlier on Mondays but opened an hour earlier on Tuesdays, or closed on a different day, and which days should have their working hours changed? Measure your sales and the number of chairs used and the times, and you will know. Then you can make the money-making adjustments and test different options. That's what experts do. That's what big business does. Measure, change, test, experiment, EVOLVE.

Our businesses are either growing or dying, evolving or dying. What used to work doesn't work so well anymore. We have to change with the times, give our customers what they want, not what we think they want or what we think they SHOULD want. Let them tell you. ASK them what they want, how you can improve your service.

All Costs Should Be Measured.

One of my clients who had a lovely restaurant thought she could save money by stopping the weekly delivery of a big, beautiful bunch of fresh flowers that stood proudly in the lobby. It was the first thing you saw when you walked into her restaurant and it was very impressive. Fortunately, she measured everything, and she found that in the first week of having no flowers (cost $120) she lost $500 in sales. So she immediately replaced the order for flowers and got them back. Sales immediately shot back up again. If she wasn't measuring, she might have blamed the weather or not even noticed the drop in sales. Don't skimp on the wrong things. Don't skimp on decent coffee or tea for your clients. They will notice the small things.

Salons should be spotlessly CLEAN. If you're using $100 per hour earning potential stylists to do $10 per hour cleaning, think again. Don't have a High I doing a High C job. They will make mistakes and that costs time and money. Is every staff member really necessary? Are they productive? Do you measure that? When you Joint Venture to cross promote services with another business, you can measure how many people show up in your salon because of that cross promotion, so you will know whether to repeat it or not. It's easy – just ask every new client where she heard about you, who invited her, where she got her Gift Certificate from. Plus, every Gift Certificate should bear the name of the presenter - "With the Compliments of..."

Every Client's Client File should have a list of the times they had appointments and how much they spent on products and services and what they bought. There are many Point Of Sale systems that work perfectly with cash registers to record all of this. But if you never look at it and analyze and compare it, you will never know what is working and what isn't working, so you won't make more money. You'll be shooting in the dark.

When you measure and monitor client performance, you can gauge how valuable the client is to you in terms of money spent in the salon, regularity of visits, amount of valuable / buying referrals, and loyalty; you can start recognizing Preferred Clients with a special lapel pin, framed certificate, special recognition at your client loyalty parties, gifts, and so on. Treating all your clients as equal in spite of the fact that some are a lot more valuable to you than others means you're not measuring and not aware of this. Look after your best people, or some other salon will.

Monitor the Language in the Salon

Do you have a Swear Box in the salon – people pay a one dollar fine every time they cuss? Do you listen to the way stylists converse with their customers – are they talking about themselves or the customer? We should talk primarily about the client – her needs, goals, fears, family, hair, problems, aspirations, pets – and make notes about that when she leaves so that we can catch up fast when she returns. You can measure this by listening and then checking her notes. You can't manage people when you hide in your office or you're never there, or when you're so busy working with your own clients that you neglect your management duties. Many salon owners make that mistake. The goal should be to work towards working "ON" your business instead of "IN" your business.

Is there pessimism or optimism in the salon – complaining and criticizing or gratitude and compliments? Do you monitor and record "for customer service purposes" all phone calls? Do you use closed circuit TV in the salon?

$$$$$$$$$$$$$$$$$$$$$$$$$$$$$

"People always ask me how long it takes to do my hair. I don't know, I'm never there."
~ Dolly Parton

Measuring can increase the ROI of a single print ad by up to 400%. It has helped me increase clients' bottom lines by many millions of dollars over the years. It works and it's well worth the effort. And it makes it infinitely easier to sell your business for a great price.

Phase Four
All About PROFIT:
Add the Magical Back End

What do I mean by the Back End? Simply put, it is commissions paid to you by other businesses – this is 100% profit and it represents 90% of my income; the rest is from coaching, training, and speaking engagements. When I talk about business partnering, strategic alliances, collaborative marketing, reciprocal marketing, joint ventures – this is what I am referring to: generating income from other businesses in the form of commissions on sales made by them as a result of your efforts. After specializing in this for 25 years and doing it long before that in the hotel and restaurant business as a manager and employee, I have yet to find a more inclusive, intelligent, leveraged, and sophisticated way to make money.

Think of a restaurant, which has a 32% food cost and a lot of other expenses and overhead. A restaurant only has about a 16% net profit, on average. When a restaurant earns a commission for referring one of its customers to another business, that commission isn't 16% - it's 100%. The same goes for your salon. It's nicer to receive commissions that entail very little work and time, no cost and no risk, and have some other business carry the costs and risk, and get to keep 100% of whatever the commission is, isn't it?

Okay, so let's put that to work in YOUR salon.

All business owners know that there is a cost to acquiring a new customer – an Acquisition Cost. The marketing and advertising cost. Most smart business owners would prefer to pay for results – that is a commission on sales made – than promises, that is advertising and marketing that may, or may not work. And they would prefer 90% of something (after paying a 10% commission) than 100% of nothing.

We have discussed Gift Certificates at length. The Gift Certificate offers a sample, a taste, a way to get to know whether or not the recipient wants more of the service or product being provided. Very soft sell – a gift. Nothing for sale. If, however, that Gift Certificate results in a sale or many sales, the business making the sales should pay the person distributing the Gift Certificates a commission on those sales. The commission is their Acquisition Cost.

For example, Mrs. Foote comes in for a cut and colour, and the salon owner or stylist enthusiastically presents her with a Gift when she leaves: a Gift Certificate for a free Jewelry cleaning and evaluation at Diamond Star Jewelers around the corner. Mrs.

Foote pops into the jeweler, and while she waits for the evaluation and cleaning of her rings and bracelets, she peruses the jewelry and buys a nice necklace for $300. The Jeweler knows who gave Mrs. Foote the Gift Certificate, because it says, "With the Compliments of Sibelle's Salon" on the Gift Certificate, so he sends the salon owner a commission check for 10% of the sale, that is $30, with a note detailing the source of the commission.

That $30 commission is pure profit to the salon – we made money by giving away a gift to one of our dear clients. Even if the Gift Certificate was never used, or if Mrs. Foote didn't buy anything, the Jewelry store got free advertising, we boosted our customer loyalty at no cost, and Mrs. Foote is happy. Win / Win / Win. No cost or risk. Just a few cents of cleaning material and the printing of the Gift Certificate (which the Jeweler pays for.)

Let's do the math: If you give each and every client who comes into the salon, every day, as well as every guest at your hair shows, one valuable Gift Certificate that can result in at least a $50 commission to you, what will happen to your bottom line? Especially with recurring commissions, for example I pay $100 per month for coaching clients who pay me the minimum $1,000 per month. That's $100 per month to your bottom line per coaching client you send me.

I recently received a $4,400 commission for a referral. How many haircuts will it take to earn that in net profit? It took me five minutes on the phone. I have a Realtor who pays $500 for a referral to someone who buys or sells a house, so when someone tells me they're thinking of buying or selling, I simply send them an email introducing them to my friend Barrie, the Realtor.

90% of my income is commissions from other businesses. Much of it is triangulated joint ventures, in other words I connect A with B and I broker the deal.

In the case of a Hair Salon, it is imperative that your stylists and employees get taught how to present and explain each Gift Certificate. Just handing one over seldom works; people don't understand, they think there's a catch, or they think it's an advertisement. Every week, the stylists should have a new Gift Certificate they're giving out.

They should understand exactly how it works: "We are gifting each client with one free tennis lesson this week, valued at $90! If you would like to take a lesson, simply call this number on your Gift Certificate, talk with Cathy, and she'll arrange your free lesson. No charge – we've taken care of that for you. There's no obligation to buy any more lessons. You can, if you like, but we just want you to have a great time with our compliments."

If your employees understand which words to use, they'll sell the idea very well. This should be part of their Job Description: "Give every client one Gift Certificate." It has to be a system – it has to happen every single time. Just think of the number of Gift Certificates you can get – all the printing paid for by the business providing the sample – all kinds of lessons (modelling, sword fighting, cooking, self defence, shooting, archery, singing, piano, makeup, and so on), consultations by Interior Designers (mine pays an average commission of $5,000!), services by accountants, dentists, chiropractors, landscapers, high end spas, furnishers, contractors, handymen, clothing stores, jewellers, and on and on and on.

If a client already has a Gift Certificate for that, give her another one, but only one per person, and only one per visit. You can even have the owner of the business issuing and printing the Gift Certificates stop by the salon to explain more about his business, and perhaps have the stylists and other employees try it out for themselves, so they love it even more. They will then be more effective and enthusiastic when they hand over the Gift Certificates.

"Suddenly I realized a trip to the salon could be about much more than just a haircut or dye job, and that the psychology is sometimes more important than the actual hairdressing. When people are going through shxx, they tell their hairdressers secrets they won't share with anyone else, and often the revelation of those secrets changes the person and how they feel about themselves. It makes them feel renewed, like confessing to their priest."
~ Tabatha Coffey

Here's How to Elicit Gift Certificates:

You approach a local Tennis Coach and ask him this question:

You: Would you prefer to have 90% of a sale you wouldn't have had, or 100% of nothing?

Coach: What do you mean?

You: Well, this may be for you, or not, no matter, let me run it by you anyway. We're looking for great services that we can introduce our clients to. We serve about [100] clients a week, and we would like to take one week to offer them each a free tennis coaching session. If they agree to continue with the classes, you pay me 10% of everything they pay you, ongoing. All you need to do is provide me with 150 Gift Certificates – I'll show you what to print on them – and we will start. I only deal with one service provider in each industry, and because I know you / trust you / shared a prison cell with you / am married to you / was referred to you by Jonathan, I would like to give you the first option to accept.

If you do, I will need the Gift Certificates by [date] and I would like you to come in to my salon and explain what you do to my staff, so they can sell your service more effectively. Perhaps offer them each a free lesson, too. What do you think?

Here's How to Present This Idea to Your Employees:

People, I have exciting news for everyone! How would you like to have more clients?

How would you like to increase the amount of your tips?

How would you like to increase the loyalty of your clients, and have them come back more frequently?

How would you like to make it easier to get more referrals from your clients?

Well, we have a new system that has been proven, and it works. From [July 1], you will be able to GIVE EACH CLIENT A GIFT valued at $50 or more! AND a different gift every time they come into the salon!

No other salon is doing that in our area, and this will attract more clients, even clients from other salons. Everyone likes to get a free mystery gift, right? Do you think this will increase your tips and the frequency of their visits? Do you think your clients will be more loyal? How about getting more referrals? Well, let me explain how it works.

You will be able to give out free, no-obligation Gift Certificates for things like lessons, interior design and landscaping advice, free manicures and pedicures, facials, spa treatments, and so on, all valued at $50 or more. And we will try to get the business owners who issue these Gift Certificates to come into the salon and briefly tell us more about what they do, to make it even more exciting.

And guess what? YOU will also get these Gift Certificates every week for yourselves! Yes, YOU will also get the value! Free! I'll explain exactly what you should say to each client at the end of her service when you give her or him their gift - just before they pay and tip!

In this way, we will add massive value to our service and attract more clients and get them spending more and coming back more frequently and referring more of their friends to us. And you will be getting them too, as my special gift to you.

Important Note: The commissions resulting from gift certificates go to the salon, not to the stylists. You did the work and set the thing up, and you get the commissions.

"I'm a beautician, not a magician. My comb is not a wand!"

Epilogue

I know you're worried. "What if all the salons use these same ideas and we're just one of many again? The market will be flooded with these ideas! Oh, woe is me!" Well, the reality is, that after presenting my ideas for 25 years in seminars, coaching sessions, conventions, key note speeches, talks, books, articles, conference calls, webinars, newsletters, and the like, I can assure you that:

1. Very few people actually implement these ideas, and
2. Very few of the people who actually implement them continue to implement them.

I always say, you can get free soap, but there are still a lot of smelly people around. It's just human nature. 57% of people are so lazy they don't even finish reading the books they start reading.

But if you're SERIOUS about success, motivated, and hungry, and you implement everything and test it and tweak it until it works great for you, you will be very grateful that you bought this cheap little booklet written by an ugly little man. For example, if you enthusiastically, consistently invite good people in for a free haircut, you will keep your chairs filled within a week of starting, and if you provide great service to the right people, more and more of those freebies will result in loyal, grateful clients. The speed at which it all happens depends entirely on YOU, and your commitment and enthusiasm.

Motivate your employees, get them on board, and the sky is the limit.

Every Salon Owner Should Read This:

Napoleon Hill once asked Andrew Carnegie, "Some people feel that you gained your fortune at the expense of those who worked for you. Will you explain your conception of the reason for the great difference between your financial achievements, and those of the men who work for you?"

Carnegie answered, in part:

"Ask me to explain the reason for the great difference between my financial achievements and the financial status of those who work for me. I can only answer you by saying that I've accumulated great wealth because I was willing to assume great responsibilities and deliver service of a widespread nature.

"Of the thousands of men who work for me, I hazard the guess that not more than a score of them would be willing to assume my

responsibilities and work the hours that I work, if I gave him all the money I possess for doing so. A few of the men who work for me have been willing to assume such responsibilities, and it is significant that every one of these is as rich as he desires to be. . . .

"I never set the wage scale of any man who works for me. Every man sets his own wage scale, by the sort of service he renders – the quality and the quantity of his service, plus the mental attitude in which he renders it. Understand this truth and you will know that there is no injustice in connection with the difference between the fortunes which men accumulate."
~ Don Watkins.

Now, read "Atlas Shrugged" and/or "The Virtue of Selfishness" by Ayn Rand. These two books have helped many of my clients to become more successful. And read my book, "Break Free!"

I leave you with my own personal mantra or slogan from Paul J. Meyer: *"Whatever you vividly imagine, ardently desire, sincerely believe, and enthusiastically act upon, must inevitably come to pass."*

Where to From Here?

1. Check out my coaching service at www.LeverageAdvantage. com – an excellent ROI and a way to avoid many costly mistakes and save a lot of time. Reading this book and trying to implement the ideas without my coaching is quite possible, but you can supercharge your progress with coaching. Contact me for a complimentary discussion to see if there's a fit for you. This offer is subject to availability – I accept a limited amount

of coaching clients from $1,000 per month:
robin@leverageadvantage.com

2. I also pay a 10% referral fee for coaching clients and paid speaking gigs. Get me involved with a hair product company and you can earn serious commissions from me.

3. If you would like to resell this booklet, we can discuss that, too.

SOME TESTIMONIALS

"For those who had never before seen or heard a dynamic delivery [at the Wella Hair Show] from that motivational fundi, Robin Elliott, it was a gratifying experience."
- SA Hairdressing & Beauty Culture.

"There has been a growth in sales of over 50%"
- Angela Lewis, Ahead of Hair.

"The new Salon Development Director for Redken, Robin Elliott, is well known for his salon training and has achieved great results in improving profits, higher sales and staff motivation."
- Hair and Beauty magazine.

"After only two months, we have experienced tremendous growth."
- Thomas Jewell, Straight A-Head

"Our weekly sales have increased from an average of $7,500 to an unprecedented $13,799 in one week. Invaluable! Any business that desires success, should make use of Robin's services."
- Rowland Harvey, Rowland's Hair Design.

"The knowledge and guidance we have acquired over the past months will always be well utilized. Thanks for your tremendous input and support."
- Giovanni Battista, Hair and Beauty.

"The sales of products has doubled and it's the highest it's been since we started business."
- Brian Steward, Hair Centre.

CONTACT INFORMATION

WEBSITE: www.LeverageAdvantage.com
– Sign up for my free weekly newsletter for business owners.

EMAIL: robin@leverageadvantage.com
– Put Your Salon Book in the Subject Line and include your full name when emailing me, please.

LINKEDIN: http://ca.linkedin.com/in/robinjelliott

BLOG: http://www.RobinJElliott.com

Thank you very much for investing in and reading my booklet. Remember, the more you learn, the more you earn! If you re-read the book in the future, you will learn new things, since your circumstances will have changed. You may even be in a new business. The information here is timeless, and it applies to most businesses, not just hair salons. I wish you every success, and we both know that success is a matter of sowing and reaping. I recommend you sow abundantly.

At the time of writing, I am available for limited, paid speaking, training, and coaching.

Robin J. Elliott
Vancouver, Canada. May 15, 2013

www.ingramcontent.com/pod-product-compliance
Lightning Source LLC
Chambersburg PA
CBHW021915190326
41519CB00008B/789